MW01135741

Is Life a Random Walk?

Is Life a Random Walk?

Harold Klemp

ECKANKAR
Minneapolis
www.Eckankar.org

Is Life a Random Walk?

Printed in USA.
Third Printing—2009
ISBN: 978-1-57043-172-2

Library of Congress Cataloging-in-Publication Data

Klemp, Harold.
　Is life a random walk? / Harold Klemp.
　　p. cm.
　ISBN 1-57043-172-8 (saddle stitch : alk. paper)
　　1. Spiritual life--Eckankar (Organization) I. Title.
BP605.E3 K559 2001
299'.93--dc21
　　　　　　　　　　　　　　　　　　　　　2001040469

♾ This paper meets the requirements ANSI/NISO Z39.48-1992 (Permanence of Paper).

Introduction

Is life just a random walk? Some analysts think so about the stock markets. Perhaps this bias is a spillover from their take on life. Who knows?

Others, myself among them, say life follows a natural order. It is predictable. While history may not repeat in an exact pattern as to place or time, the present often is a rhyme to past events.

What do you think?

If you have a strong desire to find a better, more direct way to God, read on. The truth you seek may be at your fingertips.

Is Life a Random Walk?

I was in the post office when a father entered with his young daughter. The toddler started to run back and forth in the lobby, clutching a key.

When I went to my box for the mail, the little girl followed and watched with an intent gaze as I put a key into the lock and unlocked it. She seemed fascinated by the process. It was apparent she had tried her key in several boxes without success.

Key of Opportunity

She stood and stared as I relocked my mailbox. By then her dad had finished his business and was ready to leave.

Scooping up his little girl, he made for the door, then turned back and said, "When you're that age and you've got a key, the whole world is a lock."

I thought about it, trying to learn the spiritual message. It is this: The whole world is a grand opportunity, a mystery for a child, something to unlock with a key, to discover what's there.

Do you have such a key? How does it work?

A Search for Answers

Who am I? What am I? Why am I here? Where am I going? When? And how?

Questions, questions—but good ones.

In search of answers to these questions, you come face-to-face with the very secrets of life and death. You unearth the true knowledge that has eluded the most learned scholars of mainline religions.

Even now you stand at the foot of a new ladder of discovery.

What are the ancient teachings of ECK? What do they involve? Can they improve your life? Make you a better person? These are all questions you may well ask yourself someday. Maybe today.

Help Me Remember
What God Is Like

During the mass destruction of Hurricane Andrew in August 1992, many people in southern Florida lost their homes and all belongings. Some ECKists also felt the bite of its destruction. One such ECK family accepted shelter with another family until money from the insurance company let them set up housing again.

Their hosts told a story about their four-year-old girl and a brand-new baby in the family. Soon after bringing the newborn home from the hospital, the hosts' little girl made a request. Could she please spend a few moments alone with the baby? At first the parents felt reluctance. Afraid of sibling rivalry, they wondered if she might harm the infant. But the four-year-old kept begging them to leave the nursery and let her stay with the newborn.

The parents gave in, but only after turning up the volume on the nursery intercom.

(Trust in God, but turn up the intercom.)

They listened from another room, prepared to rush back in if needed. Instead of distressed cries, however, they heard their daughter's soft voice address the infant. Her words were like a prayer.

"Baby," she said, "help me remember what God is like. I'm beginning to forget."

Many children do, in fact, remember what God is like—at least until they enter school at age three, four, or five. Then the memory begins to cloud over. Good schooling teaches them to be responsible adults in society, of course. Yet at the same time a priceless gift is lost—a child's understanding of God.

Straight Answers

Whatever your chosen religion or belief, that choice is necessary for you at this stage of your journey home to God. That's why you hold to it.

Your religion or belief is a valuable and important part of you because it reflects all your experiences from past lives.

Our spiritual heritage is far richer than a single lifetime could ever produce, the real reason many enter this life with a special gift or talent without the apparent need for learning it. Some kids even reincarnate with the knowledge of a foreign language which their siblings lack. Parents who treat reincarnation as foolish may simply dismiss such a gift with an airy, "Oh, well, he sure didn't get it from us," and let it go at that.

They have no inkling as to where or how the child picked up such an ability.

Learning the Spiritual Laws

Whenever I look at a child, I see a little adult. Mighty oaks from acorns grow. There's no impulse to talk down to children once you realize they are Souls returned from an older time and place. They need today's leg of their spiritual journey, too, the same as you and me.

Sometimes they reincarnate to wield the sword of fear or power, while at other times they come to demonstrate the Law of Love.

A child of three, four, or five will display a unique personality, perhaps an outgoing or adventurous one. But by age eight to ten, the child may suddenly turn shy and reserved. Upon reflection you'd say it isn't the same individual.

A young child often remembers the distant past and may well speak of it.

A good question to ask a child of two to four is this: What did you do when you were big? You could be surprised if the child, in a nonchalant manner, sketches out a past life in broad details. Recognize it for that.

When people leave this physical life, they ascend to the next heaven, the Astral Plane. Some advance to a higher place, the second or third heaven. The second is the Causal Plane. St. Paul spoke of a third heaven. It is one of the regions in the upper worlds where Souls go to rest, to learn different facets of spiritual law—including the Law of Love.

The books of ECK present these planes and laws in some detail.

How Children Enter a New Life

After a short or lengthy rest in the higher worlds, we return to earth as a tiny babe. The body is a new prison of sorts.

This containment of Soul is the hardest part of reincarnation to deal with. In the last physical incarnation an individual was perhaps an adult in a well-trained, functioning body. Now, with baby fingers, he will try to pick up objects but fail in the attempt. Eyes struggle to focus and make sense of a blurry world, but for some time a scene remains a smear of black-and-white shadings. Months pass, and a perception of color dawns. Little by little, the infant's mind develops in a heroic way to influence the brain to put it all together.

In effect, the mind commands the brain, "OK, now sort out the light waves and make order from chaos."

Of course, as our true, eternal Self—Soul—we exist beyond the human mind. From the lofty heights of Soul, we flash marching orders to our mind, which, in turn, passes them down the chain of command to our physical brain for execution. And so the will develops. We thus move and act. We grow.

With the passage of time, the infant comes to recognize Mommy and Daddy, vague forms that begin to register as real objects. It knows when the bottle's on the way, and so forth. A baby thus learns to put things into categories or files.

Its growing ability to place a thing into a familiar slot reduces the infant's fear, making the world a more comfortable place.

* * *

A mother observed the way her young child characterized things and put them into categories of his own making. Around the age of ten months, he began to mimic certain sounds. Sometime later, the mother noticed that every time they passed a body of water or a drinking fountain, he would say, "Mo."

One day she figured it out.

She had been teaching him to drink water from a glass. After each sip, she would ask, "More?" The child had taken the characteristics of this wet stuff in the glass and put it into the wrong file. He thought its name was "more." So anytime he saw water, he tried to call it by that name.

A child learns bit by bit. First on its

10

agenda is the name of basic things—how to identify the concrete objects in the world around him.

How Do I Get God's Love?

Over time, children pick up the finer subtleties of getting along with others. If they have the good fortune of loving parents, they soon realize that as one gets love, he must also give it. Love is like water in that only so much of it fits into a glass. Before more can go in, some must be let out. So, if one doesn't keep giving out love, "mo" can't come in.

People often wonder, *How do I get God's love?* You get more of it by giving of your own to others.

Spiritual School

All in all, earth is a spiritual school. Designed and set up by God, it lets each of us, each Soul in this world, learn more about becoming godlike—becoming more like God.

The whole purpose of you, me, and everyone else is to become more godlike. It is our mission, or purpose, here. It's the key to happiness.

People may believe they're here to mark time until the trumpets blow on the last day. At that point, having pursued a frivolous life, they expect the Lord to catch them up to some better world, to let them embark upon a useless and self-centered existence there too.

No. The true purpose of life here, there, or anywhere is to become a Co-worker with God.

Our past lives have brought experiences to polish us in a spiritual way. Like it or not, you are now the best and highest spiritual being you have ever been in any lifetime. Take a look at yourself. Like what you see? Fine. But if you don't like the face staring back at you in the mirror, keep in mind that this reflection is of your own creation. You are today the sum of all your thoughts, feelings, and actions in past lives.

I once said that sincere people who attend an ECK event—like an introductory talk on the Eckankar teachings—come because of some dissatisfaction with their belief or religion. Otherwise, why would they be there?

Yet they may be aware only in part of the pressing nature of their search. But Soul, the True Self, has heard and is yearning to go home.

It's simply a matter of time before a seeker's search begins in earnest—perhaps a week, a month, a year, fifty years, the next lifetime, or later—it matters not. Yet this may be the lifetime that a seeker admits, "I sense having lived many times in the past. I may be the best I've ever been, but I want more. Much more."

"I Want to Go Home"

A child we'll call Debra, for the sake of privacy, was born with a valve defect in her stomach. Doctors were at a loss whether she would outgrow the condition. All during Debra's childhood, her parents had introduced her to strangers: "Our daughter was born with a stomach defect. She doesn't keep food down very well."

Negative comments like that added an extra burden to this poor child's youth.

One day the problem reached a crisis. Debra's parents found her turning blue and rushed her to a hospital. By luck and divine grace, she pulled through. The doctors who treated her predicted that the stomach valve, which they fixed, would cause no future problems.

Now, Debra's older sister took a fiendish delight in making fun of her. Soon after Debra returned from the hospital, her sister picked a fight. Family rules kept the older girl from giving the younger one a physical beating, yet verbal abuse and name-calling did the job. They left no visible scars. On that particular day the younger girl simply got tired of the hazing and turned on her sister. She beat up her tormentor. Outraged, the elder ran and told their father. The wisdom of Solomon he had not, so he sent Debra to her room.

Debra was recovering from a serious condition, her sister had started the fight, but she's the one banished to her room. She lay weeping on the bed, crushed by the injustice of it.

"I want to go home," she cried. "I just

want to go home." In a spiritual sense her heart was saying, "I want to go home to God because of my unhappiness."

Each of us is Soul. Once we laughed and sang in the high heavens of God's pure Light and Sound—at play in the park. But without the discipline or need to serve others, we (Soul) served ourselves. So God sent us to earth for the rich experience of living in a world of duality, to suffer and enjoy extremes like heat and cold, wealth and poverty, or love and hate. It was all to learn the true nature of love.

That's our mission. The first big lesson is to learn to love ourselves.

So when young Debra cried, "I want to go home; I just want to go home," her plea was in a spiritual sense. In her abject misery the faint, but not extinguished, memory of Soul's onetime home flooded in upon her. She remembered that her true home wasn't on earth. She was but passing through.

Accept Life for What It Is

As Debra heard the sound of her own words, she snapped from her self-pity and returned to her human cage, timeless ages—yet a mere heartbeat—from bliss in the heart of God.

I am home, she realized.

This time, she didn't mean her heavenly home, but earth. Hard, merciless, uncaring earth.

"I'm as home as I'm going to get," she said aloud. "It won't get better here. So I may as well wipe my tears and plan for the day I'm old enough to leave." She stopped crying then. A key realization had stolen in upon her: Conditions might stumble along at home, but truth to tell, they were well within the limits of endurance. This suggested the need to accept her station in life.

What an important realization for a child!

The Hand of God

Debra grew up, married, and endured hardships that led to a budding maturity. Losing her firstborn son, the marriage missing a breakup by a narrow margin, and other such suffering took her to the brink of hopeless abandonment.

One day, depressed and despondent, she sought refuge in church. Catholicism was the faith of her youth. Now she had hit rock bottom. Inside the church, a prayer service was in session, and worshippers all around murmured soft prayers. At that moment, sunk in the depths of despair, she felt a hand of comfort come to rest upon her shoulder. Her eyes flew open in surprise. She glanced back to bless that gentle Soul's touch, but empty air greeted her widened eyes. No one stood near.

In a way, you could say it was the hand of God through the personage of a divine messenger. God Itself—in ECK we neither say Him nor Her—does not descend into the human theater to move among people in the normal sense.

Yet the Deity does send spiritual messengers, often perceived as angels, saints, and the like. Debra realized it in a heartbeat. A guardian angel had indeed placed a hand of reassurance and comfort upon her.

Debra's story is a wonderful example

of how you, too, may experience a gentle nudging from Divine Spirit (ECK) to help you on your journey home to God.

Even before leaving church, she knew that a gift of grace had touched her with a special blessing. This extraordinary moment of realization was the assurance of an ancient truth: life is more than a random walk. A divine presence had graced her. As a Catholic more grounded in the physical side of life than the mystical, she was startled by such a realization of grace. It'd come through the touch of a gentle, albeit invisible, hand.

Eternity Here and Now?

The years passed. In time Debra bore a second son we'll call Jim. Once grown he took an interest in spiritual things. Debra did too, though life's trials left raw wounds that begged for more time to heal. She still exercised caution about religion.

Yet her view about the next spiritual step was a childlike one. Intuition whispered that when a student is ready, the Master appears, and the resulting linkup is a most natural one. After all, hadn't she already waited years on end to discover the next step to truth after feeling the hand on her shoulder in church so long ago? What was another month or year?

Jim, however, with all the exuberance and impatience of youth, took a more direct tack. "Eternity now!" he said.

One day he was reading an ECK book, in back of which was listed a phone number. "What are you reading?" said Debra. "There's something in it about eternity here and now," he replied. "I'm going to call the number and see what I can find out."

A pleasant, cheery voice came on the line. An ECKist told of an upcoming meeting where someone would explain more about the teachings of ECK.

"I'm going," he told his mother.

Though leery of any religious teaching other than Catholicism, she decided to join him to ensure no one took advantage of her baby. "Mother, please," he said, "don't make a scene." Jim could imagine her throwing angry accusations at the group. He offered a compromise.

"If you promise not to embarrass me, you may come."

* * *

So they set out. Near the end of the introductory meeting on the teachings of ECK, a speaker addressed the group. "To give you a better idea of what I'm talking about," he said, "I would like to invite you all to sing HU with me." Then, very softly, he and the others began to chant HU.

HU is an ancient, holy name for God. You can sing it at home. Simply sit or lie in a quiet place and sing HU (pronounced like "hue"). This age-old song lets the Voice of God enter you as love, Light, or Sound.

The Light and Sound of God are integral parts of divine love known to but a few. The twin pillars of God's love, they are the mainstays of the ECK teachings. In fact, the spiritual travelers of ECK ride them out of the body and into the cosmic seas via Soul Travel, like a surfer riding ocean waves. This method is a direct route to finding love, wisdom, and spiritual freedom.

* * *

Debra's mind drifted to a time three years earlier at a Renaissance fair. Astrology and many other paths had exhibits there.

In a little room where people came to meditate stood a crystal bowl. The host had run a stick with a rubber tip along the edge of the bowl, producing a magnificent, soothing sound. It was most beautiful and healing.

* * *

So at this ECK meeting Debra listened to the others chant HU. *That sound, that sound!* Where had she heard it before? Suddenly it dawned on her: it was like the soothing sound at the fair. The stick with the rubber tip running slowly around the edge of the crystal bowl had also made this sound of HU, ancient name for God.

She learned that a recording of a HU Song was available at the ECK meeting. Full of excitement, she bought one. It surprised Jim. "What are you doing, Mother? You never buy such things."

She told him about the same wonderful sound she'd once heard at the Renaissance fair. She simply wanted to hear it once more.

A Trip to the ECK Temple

Mother and son became members of Eckankar. Soon after, the Temple of ECK opened in Chanhassen, Minnesota, a suburb of Minneapolis. "Let's drive to Minnesota and see this place," Jim said.

"Yes," she agreed. "Maybe we'll have a great experience there."

In her heart she knew she would.

This occasion sparked a dim reminder from her childhood, when she'd sobbed on the bed: "I want to go home. I just want to go home." She didn't understand what she had meant then, and even less now.

So they drove from the East Coast with a sadly out-of-date map of Minneapolis. Many changes since the map's publication had all but rendered it useless. Upon reaching the outskirts of Chanhassen, they asked a young gas station attendant for directions to the Temple of ECK.

"Never heard of it," said the youth.

Back on the road, they tracked an uncertain route to the town center of Chan-hassen, certain of finding the Temple of ECK nearby. But to complicate matters, dusk had stolen upon them. Then, while heading down the main street, a sense of déjà vu overcame Debra. She braked to a stop in the middle of the street.

"Mother!" Jim said. "What are you doing?"

Frozen in wonder at the wheel, she replied, "I've been here before!"

Long years ago, a recurring dream had foretold this visit to a small town with what seemed like a year-round winter. Except for a brief spell that natives call summer, the description fits Minnesota.

In her dreams she had walked past a hardware store, and then she would see the town clock. The scene was always the same. She'd awake to a feeling of dreams more real than waking life. Yet she'd forgotten them until this very night.

"I've been here before," she repeated. Traffic backing up behind them forced her to move on. Minutes later, they found the Temple of ECK near the edge of town.

This ECK Temple is a very special place. It's an outer symbol for the holy temple of God within the heart of all people. Visitors to it often remark upon a presence—a very definite, loving, divine one. The temple reflects and resonates with the Light and Sound of God, and many people mention this sense of being in a unique, holy place.

The Great Experience?

Parking the car, mother and son entered the ECK Temple and took seats in the sanctuary. Debra waited in quiet expectation, wondering, *When will I have my great experience?* Even as the thought arose, a soft voice from nowhere said, "Well, what do you want? Do you need to get run over by a truck?"

Already she'd forgotten the déjà vu of minutes ago.

* * *

Someone once asked me, "How do people in ECK usually find truth?" He meant: does it hit like a bombshell?

Yes, it could be an experience to deeply stir the emotions and feelings. Yet more often its subtlety slips past people. So they miss it. Within the hour, Debra had had a marvelous experience of locating the actual town from recurring dreams years long gone. That was the "great experience."

Great skeptics and doubters often go farthest on the path to God. Someone may ask, "Is there hope for me? I don't buy this God stuff." No problem; take your time, for all seekers must proceed at their own pace.

But one truth I can give you is the word *HU*, and the spiritual exercises to find God. Yet the success of these depends upon you. Can you spend a few minutes a day to open your heart to the Holy Spirit? To do the spiritual exercises with love and passion? To give your whole mind and heart to such a self-discipline for a few moments?

If the reply is yes, you are bound to make progress in your quest for the secret laws of life. Today's mysteries will no longer be mysteries tomorrow.

A Few Sounds of God

After Debra became a member of Eckankar, she learned the meaning of a buzzing sound she'd heard for years. That sound is but another of the Sounds of God. It's like a swarm of bees and originates on the Etheric Plane, region of the subconscious mind. This plane lies beyond the Mental Plane and is the highest of the spirito-material worlds. Beyond it is the Soul Plane, first of the true spiritual worlds.

She noticed this buzzing sound from the Etheric Plane because it was the level of consciousness she'd gained in past lives. Her next spiritual step was the Soul Plane. Early on in this life she'd reconnected to the Etheric Plane, as evidenced by this buzzing sound.

There was another sound.

This one was like the high, piercing note of a lone musical instrument. Though it didn't hurt the ear, it rose higher, soaring beyond the range of human hearing, lifting her to new spiritual peaks. This piercing note? Still another mode of God's Voice. All who hear such divine sounds find a purification of spirit and the blessings of the Most High. A breath of true liberty.

The Voice of God is the Holy Spirit in Its twin manifestations of Sound and Light. The more significant of the two for us is the Sound.

TV and the print media give wide coverage to the light that people often report after a near-death experience. The Light is often the earlier of the two manifestations to appear, so more people remark upon that aspect of the Holy Spirit. The Sound many times comes later.

Our focus here is on the Sound. It may be like a heavenly choir, a magnificent orchestra, or perhaps a Gregorian chant of medieval times. Again, Its echoes include such stirrings of nature as distant thunder, the rustling of leaves, the chirp of a cricket, the soft breathing of a lover, or the mewing of a kitten.

The Sound of God lifts you to new spiritual heights.

Every holy sound corresponds to a plane or subregion of God, to blend with your exact spiritual level. These sounds, listed in many of the ECK books and discourses, are like signposts. A given sound is a valuable clue to the level of consciousness you reached in a past life or reflects your divine station now.

This lifetime is a precious chance to reawaken to your true destiny. The path of ECK is the next leap to unraveling the secrets of life.

The Voice of God

What are the Sound and Light of God? What do they signify?

The Light and Sound are the Voice of God, the expression of God's love for us. They comprise the whole of God's love. Together, they are what religion calls the Holy Spirit.

In speaking of the Light, we say, "Yes, there is such a thing as the Light of God. It's a thousand times brighter than any sun, or it may be softer than the light of a golden moon."

The Light of God illumines your entire being, inside and out.

Other Sounds of God on the inner

planes may be like musical instruments, birds, choirs, machines, the ocean, high-pitched whistles, a murmur or crescendo of wind or water. Maybe the tinkling of joyous laughter. All these are holy sounds.

A word to help open your heart to God's love is *HU*. It is an old, revered name for God.

Real Love in Light and Sound

Some who hear ECKists tell of the Sound and Light of God think of familiar terms like *grace*, *faith*, or *love*. But careless use has robbed these words of their true meaning. The Sound and Light of God are the essence of the Holy Spirit instead of a description of Its attributes, like grace, faith, or love.

They are the real thing.

The Sound and Light of God are actual Light, which shines, and Sound, which echoes throughout all worlds. They uphold life.

For many seekers, the Light appears first in one of Its many forms. Often It comes in the dream state. Some see It as a blue light in the shape of a candle or globe, as a yellow or pink light, green, violet, or white light. White, for example, reflects the purity of God's love; blue shows the love of the Mahanta, also called the Inner Master. Yellow is a pure spiritual color. Pink, an indication of God's Light touching your emotions or feelings at the Astral level.

Whatever the color, It is one of the many signs of God's love for you. It is an assurance of divine grace.

It is a transforming presence for one and all.

So what do you think? Is life just a random walk? Is your spiritual life at the mercy of chance? Or is our life a spiritual path in line with some natural order or rhythm, as Debra found?

* * *

The spiritual travelers of ECK roam the cosmic worlds. They discovered their own proof about life as a journey guided by a divine hand and now exist within God's Sound and Light. So may you. The greatest of the spiritual travelers was once a seeker, perhaps like you.

And what is there to gain? A certainty of direction in life—and love.

Here's a spiritual exercise to try if you want to experience the Light or Sound of God:

Shut your eyes and look into the Spiritual Eye. (It's between your eyebrows, in the center of your forehead.) Sing HU (like "hue"), an ancient name for God, one of the most powerful words for spiritual upliftment I can give you.

As you sing HU, listen for a holy Sound. It may come in any number of ways: like the sound of a rumbling train, a singing bird, buzzing bees, a mellow flute, or even soothing guitars. It brings joy and wonder.

The holy sounds are the creative action of the Life Force, the ECK, as It moves atoms in the invisible worlds. The Sound to reach your ears resonates with your state of consciousness.

While singing HU, imagine the holy Sound of God cascading over you, like a waterfall of sparkling pure waters. It is cleansing the blemishes of spirit. This Sound Current may also impart an insight into your past behavior that is the root of a current problem today.

The Sound opens a secret path to the joys of love and grace. You find peace, joy, and spiritual freedom.

You are at a crossroads. Will you take a bold look at the Light and Sound of God as the ultimate spiritual guide?

If yes, then you are ready for the beautiful and powerful teachings of ECK. They offer the most direct route to wisdom, power, and freedom. And to love, the richest gift of all.

Let's get started.

For free information, with no obligation, you may reach us at:

- www.Eckankar.org
- 1-800-LOVE GOD
- ECKANKAR, PO Box 2000, Chanhassen, MN 55317-2000 USA.

Glossary

Words set in SMALL CAPS are defined elsewhere in this glossary.

ECK. *EHK* The Life Force, the Holy Spirit, or Audible Life Current which sustains all life.

ECKANKAR. *EHK-ahn-kahr* Religion of the Light and Sound of God. Also known as the Ancient Science of SOUL TRAVEL. A truly spiritual religion for the individual in modern times. The teachings provide a framework for anyone to explore their own spiritual experiences. Established by Paul Twitchell, the modern-day founder, in 1965. The word means "Co-worker with God."

ECK MASTERS. Spiritual Masters who can assist and protect people in their spiritual studies and travels. The ECK Masters are from a long line of God-Realized SOULS who know the responsibility that goes with spiritual freedom.

HU. *HYOO* The most ancient, secret name for God. The singing of the word *HU* is considered a love song to God. It can be sung aloud or silently to oneself.

LIVING **ECK** MASTER.   The title of the spiritual
    leader of ECKANKAR. His duty is to lead SOULS
    back to God. The Living ECK Master can
    assist spiritual students physically as the
    Outer Master, in the dream state as the
    Dream Master, and in the spiritual worlds
    as the Inner Master. SRI Harold Klemp be-
    came the MAHANTA, the Living ECK Master
    in 1981.

MAHANTA.   *mah-HAHN-tah* A title to describe
    the highest state of God Consciousness on
    earth, often embodied in the LIVING ECK
    MASTER. He is the Living Word. An expres-
    sion of the Spirit of God that is always with
    you.

PLANES.   The levels of existence, such as the
    Physical, Astral, Causal, Mental, Etheric,
    and Soul planes.

SOUL.   The True Self. The inner, most sacred
    part of each person. Soul exists before birth
    and lives on after the death of the physical
    body. As a spark of God, Soul can see, know,
    and perceive all things. It is the creative
    center of Its own world.

SOUL TRAVEL.   The expansion of consciousness.
    The ability of SOUL to transcend the physical
    body and travel into the spiritual worlds of
    God. Soul Travel is taught only by the
    LIVING ECK MASTER. It helps people unfold

34

spiritually and can provide proof of the existence of God and life after death.

SOUND AND LIGHT OF **ECK.**   The Holy Spirit. The two aspects through which God appears in the lower worlds. People can experience them by looking and listening within themselves and through SOUL TRAVEL.

SPIRITUAL EXERCISES OF **ECK.**   The daily practice of certain techniques to get us in touch with the Light and Sound of God.

SRI.   *SREE* A title of spiritual respect, similar to reverend or pastor, used for those who have attained the Kingdom of God. In ECKANKAR, it is reserved for the MAHANTA, the LIVING ECK MASTER.

For more explanations of Eckankar terms, see *A Cosmic Sea of Words: The ECKANKAR Lexicon* by Harold Klemp.

For Further Reading and Study

Past Lives, Dreams, and Soul Travel
Harold Klemp

What if you could recall past-life lessons for your benefit today? What if you could learn the secret knowledge of dreams to gain the wisdom of the heart? Or Soul Travel, to master the shift in consciousness needed to find peace and contentment? To ride the waves of God's love and mercy? Let Harold Klemp, leading authority in all three fields, show you how.

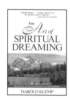

The Art of Spiritual Dreaming
Harold Klemp

Dreams are a treasure. A gift from God. Harold Klemp shows how to find a dream's spiritual gold, and how to experience God's love. Get insights from the past and future, grow in confidence, and make decisions about career and finances. Do this from a unique perspective: by recognizing the spiritual nature of your dreams.

A Modern Prophet Answers Your Key Questions about Life
Harold Klemp

A pioneer of today's focus on "everyday spirituality" shows you how to experience and understand God's love in your life—anytime, anyplace. His answers to hundreds of questions help guide you to your own source of wisdom, peace, and deep inner joy.

Autobiography of a Modern Prophet
Harold Klemp

Master your spiritual destiny. One man's journey illuminates the way. Venture to the outer reaches of the last great frontier, your spiritual destiny! The deeper you explore it, the closer you come to discovering your own divine nature as an infinite, eternal spark of God. This book leads you there!

How to Survive Spiritually in Our Times,
Mahanta Transcripts, Book 16
Harold Klemp

A master storyteller, Harold Klemp weaves stories of small

miracles and gifts from God that happen in everyday life with tools and techniques to help readers see deeper truths within and apply them to life *now*. He speaks directly to Soul, that divine, eternal spark—the Real Self. The survivor. Spiritual survival is only the starting point in one's spiritual life. Harold Klemp shows how to thrive! The Mahanta Transcripts are highlights from Harold Klemp's worldwide speaking tours.

Those Wonderful ECK Masters
Harold Klemp

Could you be one of the countless people who have been touched by a meeting with an ECK Master? These real-life stories and spiritual exercises can awaken you to the presence and help of these spiritual guides. Since the beginning of time they have offered guidance, protection, and divine love to help you fulfill your spiritual destiny.

35 Golden Keys to Who You Are & Why You're Here
Linda C. Anderson

Discover thirty-five golden keys to mastering your spiritual destiny through the ancient teachings of Eckankar,

Religion of the Light and Sound of God. The dramatic, true stories in this book equal anything found in the spiritual literature of today. Learn ways to immediately bring more love, peace, and purpose to your life.

Available from your local bookstores, online bookstores, and www.Eckankar.org. Or call (952) 380-2222, or write ECKANKAR, Dept. BK36, PO Box 2000, Chanhassen, MN 55317-2000 USA.

There May Be an Eckankar Study Group near You

Eckankar offers a variety of local and international activities for the spiritual seeker. With hundreds of study groups worldwide, Eckankar is near you! Many areas have Eckankar centers where you can browse through the books in a quiet, unpressured environment, talk with others who share an interest in this ancient teaching, and attend beginning discussion classes on how to gain the attributes of Soul: wisdom, power, love, and freedom.

Around the world, Eckankar study groups offer special one-day or weekend seminars on the basic teachings of Eckankar. For membership information, visit the Eckankar Web site (www.Eckankar.org). For the location of the Eckankar center or study group nearest you, click on "Eckankar around the World" for a listing of those areas with Web sites. You're also welcome to check your phone book under **ECKANKAR;** call (952) 380-2222, Ext. BK36; or write **ECKANKAR, Att: Information, BK36, PO Box 2000, Chanhassen, MN 55317-2000 USA.**

☐ Please send me information on the nearest Eckankar center or study group in my area.

☐ Please send me more information about membership in Eckankar, which includes a twelve-month spiritual study.

Please type or print clearly

Name _____
            first (given)   last (family)

Street _____ Apt. # _____

City _____ State/Prov. _____

Zip/Postal Code _____ Country _____

Mail this form (or a copy) to **ECKANKAR, Att: Information, PO Box 2000, Chanhassen, MN 55317-2000 USA.**

Or fax it to **(952) 380-2196** (fax line always open).

You can also find out more about Eckankar (including membership) at **www.Eckankar.org**.

About the Author

Harold Klemp was born in Wisconsin and grew up on a small farm. He attended a two-room country schoolhouse before going to high school at a religious boarding school in Milwaukee, Wisconsin.

After preministerial college in Milwaukee and Fort Wayne, Indiana, he enlisted in the U.S. Air Force. There he trained as a language specialist at Indiana University and a radio intercept operator at Goodfellow AFB, Texas. Then followed a two-year stint in Japan where he first encountered Eckankar.

In October 1981, he became the spiritual leader of Eckankar, Religion of the Light and Sound of God. His full title is Sri Harold Klemp, the Mahanta, the Living ECK Master. As the Living ECK Master, Harold Klemp is responsible for the continued evolution of the Eckankar teachings.

His mission is to help people find their way back to God in this life. Harold Klemp travels to ECK seminars in North America, Europe, and the South Pacific. He has also visited Africa and many countries throughout the world, meeting with spiritual seekers and giving inspirational talks. There are many video and audio recordings of his public talks available.

In his talks and writings, Harold Klemp's sense of humor and practical approach to spirituality have helped many people around the world find truth in their lives and greater inner freedom, wisdom, and love.

International Who's Who of Intellectuals
Ninth Edition

Reprinted with permission of Melrose Press Ltd., Cambridge, England, excerpted from *International Who's Who of Intellectuals, Ninth Edition,* Copyright 1992 by Melrose Press Ltd.